POLAND

COUNTRY EXPLORERS

Sean McCollum

Lerner Publications Company • Minneapolis

Lerner Publications Company
A division of Lerner Publishing Group, Inc.
241 First Avenue North
Minneapolis, MN 55401 U.S.A.

Website address: www.lernerbooks.com

Library of Congress Cataloging-in-Publication Data

McCollum, Sean.
    Poland / by Sean McCollum.
        p.   cm. — (Country explorers)
    Includes index.
    ISBN 978–1–58013–597–9 (lib. bdg. : alk. paper)
    1. Poland—Juvenile literature. I. Title.
    DK4147.M395 2009
    943.8—dc22   2008012677

Manufactured in the United States of America
1 2 3 4 5 6 – PA – 14 13 12 11 10 09

Table of Contents

Welcome!

On a map, Poland looks a bit like the head of a lion. (Its long, shaggy mane can be found at the bottom of the map in the south.) Poland is in the continent of Europe. The Baltic Sea rests to the north of Poland. Lithuania and a small piece of Russia sit to the north and east. Belarus is at Poland's eastern border. Ukraine, Slovakia, and the Czech Republic lie to the south. Germany is to the west.

Poland

GERMANY

The Baltic Sea laps at a beach along the coast of Poland.

BALTIC
SEA

N

GULF OF
GDANSK

KALININGRAD
(RUSSIA)

LITHUANIA

Gdansk

COASTAL LOWLANDS

POMERANIAN
LAKES

MASURIAN
LAKES

BELARUS

LAKE   REGION

BIALOWIEZA
FOREST

VISTULA RIVER

CENTRAL   PLAINS

Poznan

Warsaw ★

POLAND

Lodz

ODER RIVER

POLISH UPLANDS

SUDETEN MTNS

CZECH
REPUBLIC

Wroclaw

mountains

plains

uplands

lowlands

★ country's capital

Krakow

Auschwitz

Wieliczka

MILES

0   50   100

0   50   100   150

KILOMETERS

CARPATHIAN MOUNTAINS

RYSY
PEAK

SLOVAKIA

UKRAINE

High Land

The Vistula River starts in the Carpathian Mountains. The river winds north through forests. The mountains become rolling hills when the river reaches the Polish Uplands.

The Carpathian Mountains and surrounding forest in southern Poland

Map Whiz Quiz

Take a look at the map on page 5. Trace the outline of Poland onto a piece of paper. Can you find Germany? Mark this side of your map with a *W* for west. How about Belarus? Mark this side with an *E* for east. Color the Baltic Sea and the Vistula River blue.

A tour boat heads toward Wawel Castle on the Vistula River near Krakow, Poland.

This part of the Lake Region is in northeastern Poland.

Keep Heading North

The Vistula River soon leaves the Polish Uplands. It travels across the Central Plains. Farther north, the river flows through woods and hills in the Lake Region.

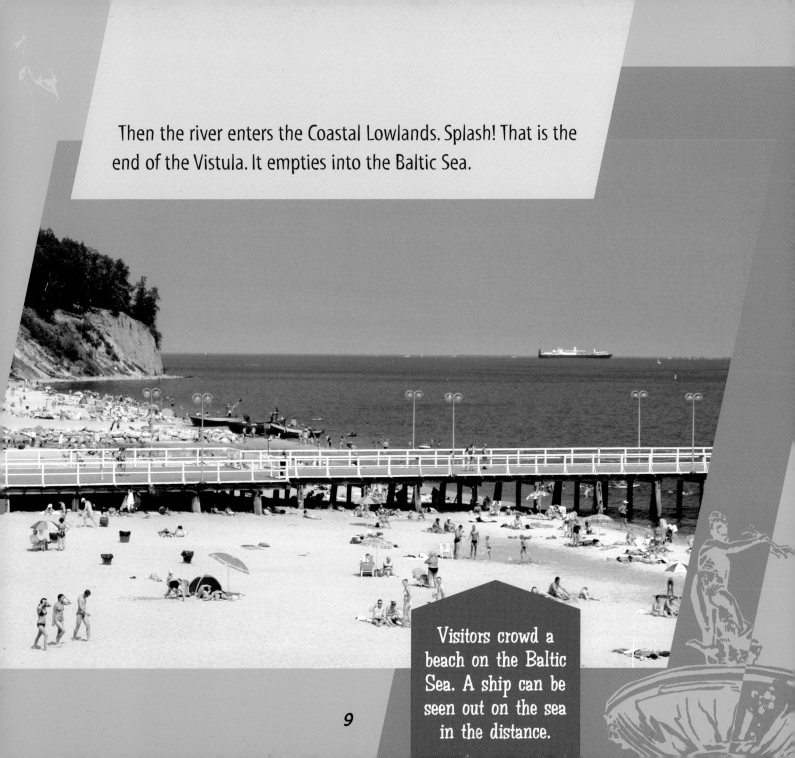

Then the river enters the Coastal Lowlands. Splash! That is the end of the Vistula. It empties into the Baltic Sea.

9

Visitors crowd a beach on the Baltic Sea. A ship can be seen out on the sea in the distance.

Polish Roots

Most Poles belong to the ethnic group known as Slavs. More than two thousand years ago, some Slavs settled in what has become modern-day Poland. They were called the Polanie. That word means "people of the plains." The Polanie are the long-ago relatives of modern-day Poles.

Many Polish people are related to their country's long-ago settlers the Polanie.

A Polish Legend

A Polish legend tells of Poland's first settler. Long ago, three brothers—Rus, Czech, and Lech—were searching for a place to live. They saw a white eagle building a nest. "Good idea," thought Lech. He decided this beautiful, green spot would be his home. That land became Poland. Rus ended up in Russia. And Czech went to the Czech Republic. The white stripe on the Polish flag stands for the white eagle.

This Polish family lives in the country in central Poland.

Poland's People

Many Poles have light skin and brown or blond hair. Almost all of them are ethnic Poles. That means their families stem from the ancient Polanie people. Only a small number of Polish families have other ethnic backgrounds.

These Polish girls sit in kindergarten class.

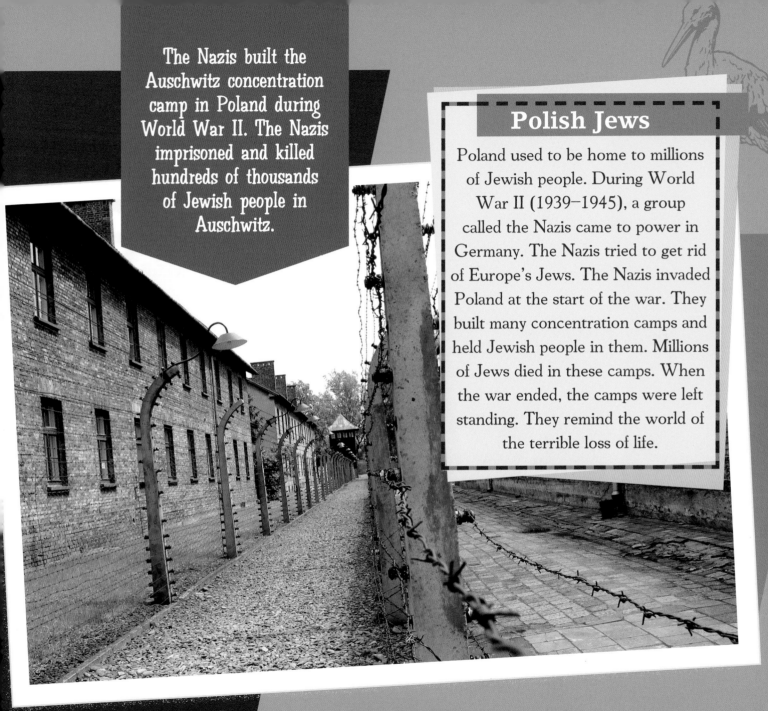

The Nazis built the Auschwitz concentration camp in Poland during World War II. The Nazis imprisoned and killed hundreds of thousands of Jewish people in Auschwitz.

Polish Jews

Poland used to be home to millions of Jewish people. During World War II (1939–1945), a group called the Nazis came to power in Germany. The Nazis tried to get rid of Europe's Jews. The Nazis invaded Poland at the start of the war. They built many concentration camps and held Jewish people in them. Millions of Jews died in these camps. When the war ended, the camps were left standing. They remind the world of the terrible loss of life.

Tough Times

European countries have often fought over land. Invaders came over the Baltic Sea and Central Plains of Poland. Foreign rulers gained control of Poland many times. After World War II, the Polish Communist Party gained control of the government.

People in Warsaw, Poland, stand in line for food in 1980.

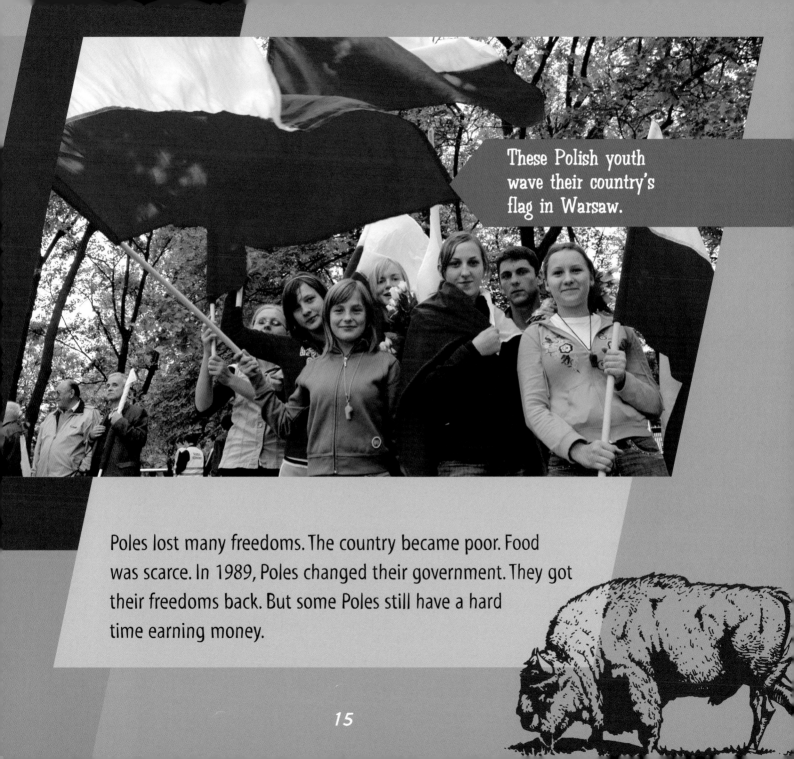

These Polish youth wave their country's flag in Warsaw.

Poles lost many freedoms. The country became poor. Food was scarce. In 1989, Poles changed their government. They got their freedoms back. But some Poles still have a hard time earning money.

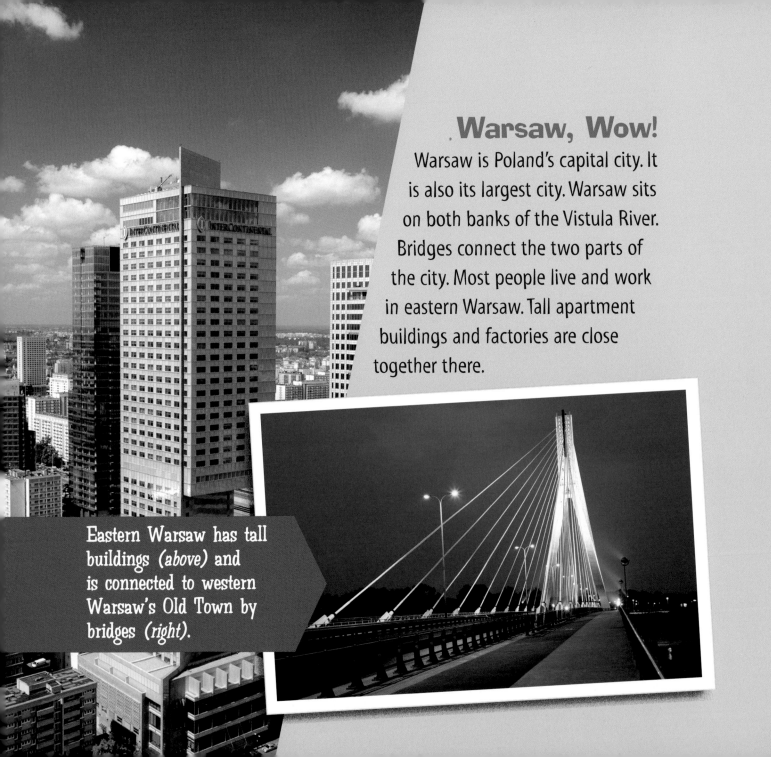

Warsaw, Wow!

Warsaw is Poland's capital city. It is also its largest city. Warsaw sits on both banks of the Vistula River. Bridges connect the two parts of the city. Most people live and work in eastern Warsaw. Tall apartment buildings and factories are close together there.

Eastern Warsaw has tall buildings (*above*) and is connected to western Warsaw's Old Town by bridges (*right*).

People sit at outdoor cafés in the Old Town part of Warsaw.

Old Town is in western Warsaw. The city began there hundreds of years ago. New Town is next to Old Town. But New Town is only a little newer. Most of Warsaw's buildings were destroyed in World War II. After the war, builders remade lots of historic structures in Old Town.

Religion

Almost all Poles are Christians. Most of them belong to the Roman Catholic Church. On Sundays, Catholics fill the streets. They are going to Mass, their religious service. At about the age of eight, kids celebrate their First Holy Communion.

Members attend Mass at a Catholic church in a village in north-eastern Poland.

A group of Polish girls are wearing their white dresses to celebrate their First Holy Communion.

This is a big day! The children take part in the whole church service for the first time. Relatives come from far away to celebrate. Some Polish Christians are members of the Eastern Orthodox and Protestant churches. A small number of Poles are Jewish.

Polish Pope

Pope John Paul II (1920–2005) was the first Polish pope. The pope is the head of the Roman Catholic Church. John Paul became pope in 1978. (He is shown below in a picture from 2002.) People all over Poland ran into the streets to celebrate. Pope John Paul II loved his homeland very much. The Polish people felt great pride.

Language

The sound of two Poles talking might seem like whispering. That's because Polish has a few specials sounds. Polish speakers make lots of *sh*, *ch*, and *zh* sounds. The Polish language uses the same basic alphabet that English does. But some letters have an accent mark above them. Other letters have a hook underneath them. The accent marks show speakers when to make the special sounds.

A group of people walk through Constitution Square in Warsaw.

20

FRYZJER KOSM ETYKA SOLA

What Does It Say?

Most Polish words are not familiar to English speakers. But a few Polish words come from English words. Do you know what *telefon*, *plastyk*, and *guma* mean? (If you guessed "telephone," "plastic," and "gum," you are right!)

kuchnie & wnętrza

www.kuchniefan
tel. 741 60

This shopping mall in Poland has groceries (*spozywczy*), cosmetics (*kosmetyka*) and kitchen and interior furniture (*kuchnie* and *wnetrza*).

21

City Life

Most Poles live in cities. City kids usually live in large buildings. The buildings are full of apartments. Newer apartments are much the same as those in U.S. cities. In the suburbs, many people have larger houses with yards.

Far left. This apartment building is in Warsaw. Many families live in apartments in the city. But some live in houses in the suburbs, like this one outside Gdansk *(left).*

Under Communist rule, few people had houses. Most lived in apartments. A whole family fit into a small living space. Apartments often had two rooms—a bedroom and a living room. A cooking area was tucked into a corner. Two or three families might have shared a bathroom.

These children play in an apartment in Poland. Many families still live in apartments. But life is very different than it was under Communist rule.

Country Life

About one out of four Poles farms the land. Farmers often grow potatoes, sugar beets, cabbage, barley, rye, and wheat. Kids help care for the family's pigs, cattle, and sheep.

A farmer plows a field in south central Poland.

In the country, people hold age-old festivals. For example, people celebrate the change of seasons. On the first day of spring, kids drown Marzanna. Marzanna is a figure that looks like a scarecrow. The scarecrow stands for winter.

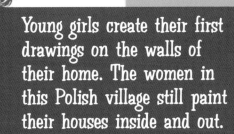

Young girls create their first drawings on the walls of their home. The women in this Polish village still paint their houses inside and out.

Family Time

Lots of city kids in Poland have just one brother or sister. Or they may be the family's only child. But in the countryside, families are larger. Sundays are family time. Grandparents, aunts, uncles, and cousins all get together.

This Polish family has two children.

All in the Family

Here are some Polish words for family members.

grandfather	dziadek	(JAH-dek)
grandmother	babcia	(BAHB-chah)
father	ojciec	(OY-chehts)
mother	matka	(MAHT-kah)
uncle (father's brother)	stryj	(str-YEE)
uncle (mother's brother)	wuj	(VOO-ee)
aunt	ciotka	(CHAHT-kah)
son	syn	(SIHN)
daughter	corka	(TSOOR-kah)
brother	brat	(BRAHT)
sister	siostra	(SHOH-strah)

Four generations of a family get together for a photo in central Poland. *Left to right:* A woman stands with her great grandson and son as her granddaughter looks on.

Time to Eat

Much Polish food is made with vegetables, grains, or meat. The food comes from Poland's farms or gardens. Family meals include lots of dark rye bread and deep red beet soup.

Borscht, a traditional beet soup, is popular in Poland.

Sauerkraut (pickled cabbage) shows up in dumplings. Sauerkraut, fresh cabbage, bacon, and sausage get mixed together in *bigos*, a favorite Polish stew.

Polish kids satisfy their sweet tooth with yummy desserts. Poppy-seed cake and *paczki* (POHNCH-kee) are two favorites. Paczki are jelly-filled doughnuts.

A girl eats paczki in front of a pastry shop in Warsaw.

Celebrations!

Poles love Christmas and Easter. These are the biggest Christian holidays. On Christmas Eve, Christian kids watch for the first star. When it appears, the family enjoys a feast. Then everyone sings carols and exchanges presents.

All Saints' Day in Warsaw

Dear Grandma,

Yesterday, November 1, was All Saints' Day. The part I liked best is an old tradition. All over Poland, people go to a graveyard. They put flowers and candles on the graves of dead family members. Then they light the candles. Thousands of twinkling candles are a beautiful sight.

See you soon!

Janie

Yo

Y

Any

At Easter, Catholic families take painted eggs to church. A priest blesses the eggs. On Easter Monday, country boys dump buckets of water on girls. But girls have buckets too. Gotcha!

Happy Name Day to You!

Polish children have name-day celebrations. Polish Catholics are often named after saints. Each day of the year is the feast day of a saint. For example, girls named Alice celebrate on June 21. That is Saint Alice Day.

Catholics wait for the priest to bless their Easter baskets.

These Polish students are taking a test.

Ready for School?

In Poland, kids begin primary school when they are seven years old. Kids go to school five days a week. Classes start at about eight o'clock. They end at two o'clock.

Kids study science, math, history, geography, social studies, Polish, English, art, and music. Older kids study computer science. After school, kids might go to music lessons. Or they might play sports.

This third-grade class poses in their school uniforms. Poland passed a law in 2007 that requires students in elementary and junior high schools to wear uniforms.

Sweet Treats

On the first day of kindergarten, kids get a special treat. Each child gets a colorful cardboard funnel. The funnel is filled with candy. Do you think that makes kids excited about going to school?

Fresh Air

Sometimes, kids go to the Bialowieza Forest on field trips. The forest used to be a private hunting ground for kings and other royalty. Some of the trees are hundreds of years old. They stand as tall as fifteen-story buildings.

Visitors look at a fallen tree in the forest.

Left: Some of the trees along Royal Oaks Way are five hundred years old. *Below*: Bison are some of the animals that roam the forest.

Horses draw carts full of kids along narrow trails. One section is called the Royal Oaks Way. Each tree there is named after a member of Polish royalty from long ago.

Lots to See

Poland is full of cool places. Wawel Castle is in Krakow. Early Polish kings used to live there. A legend says that a dragon once lived in a cave under the castle.

Wawel Castle in Krakow is on the Vistula River.

Another neat spot is deep underground at Wieliczka. Miners have carved sculptures out of salt. One room is full of carved gnomes. (In stories, gnomes were said to live underground and guard treasures.)

Amber

Items made from amber are popular in Poland. Amber is the hardened sap of pine trees. The trees grew long ago near the Baltic Sea. Artists make amber jewelry. Some amber has prehistoric bugs inside. Thousands of years ago, the insects got caught in the sticky sap before it hardened.

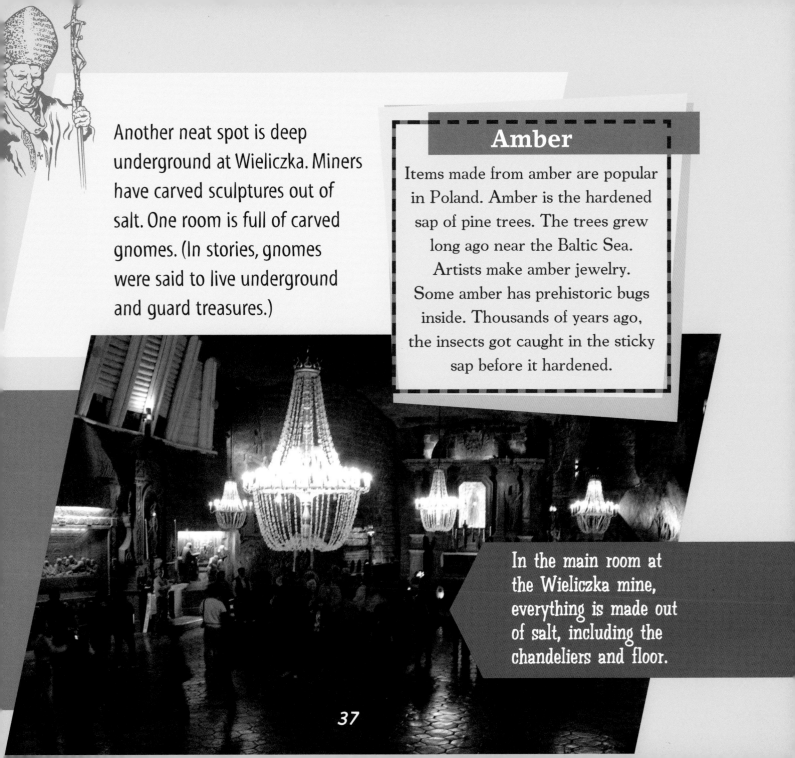

In the main room at the Wieliczka mine, everything is made out of salt, including the chandeliers and floor.

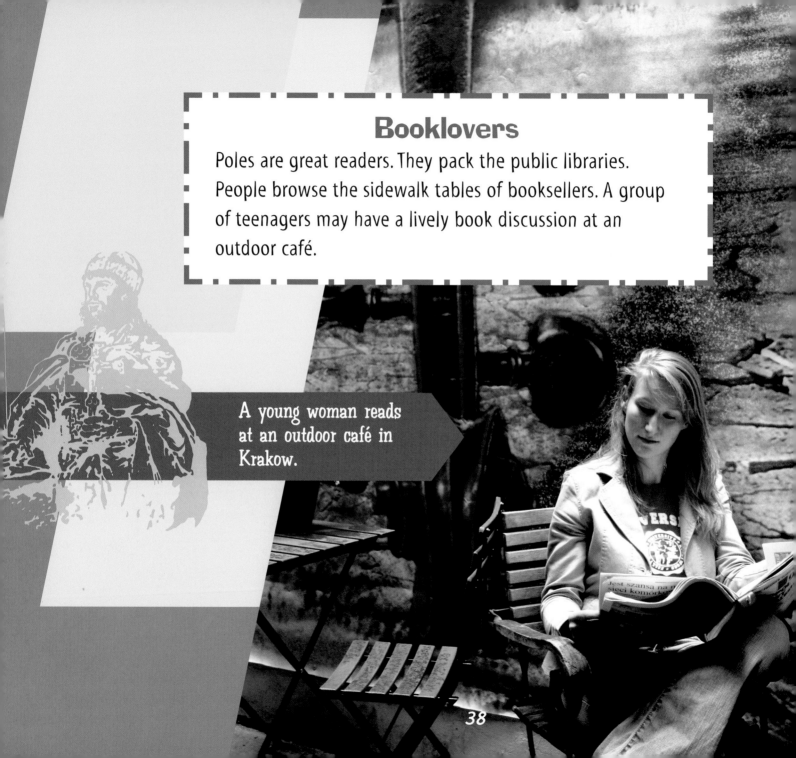

Booklovers

Poles are great readers. They pack the public libraries. People browse the sidewalk tables of booksellers. A group of teenagers may have a lively book discussion at an outdoor café.

A young woman reads at an outdoor café in Krakow.

Poles are great writers too. Each year, one writer worldwide wins the Nobel Prize in literature. This prize is one of the most respected honors in the world. During the 1900s, five Polish writers won this award.

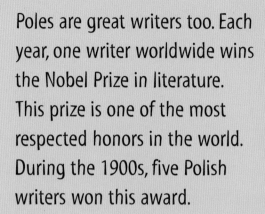

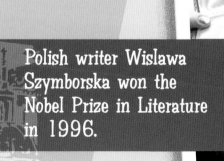

Polish writer Wislawa Szymborska won the Nobel Prize in Literature in 1996.

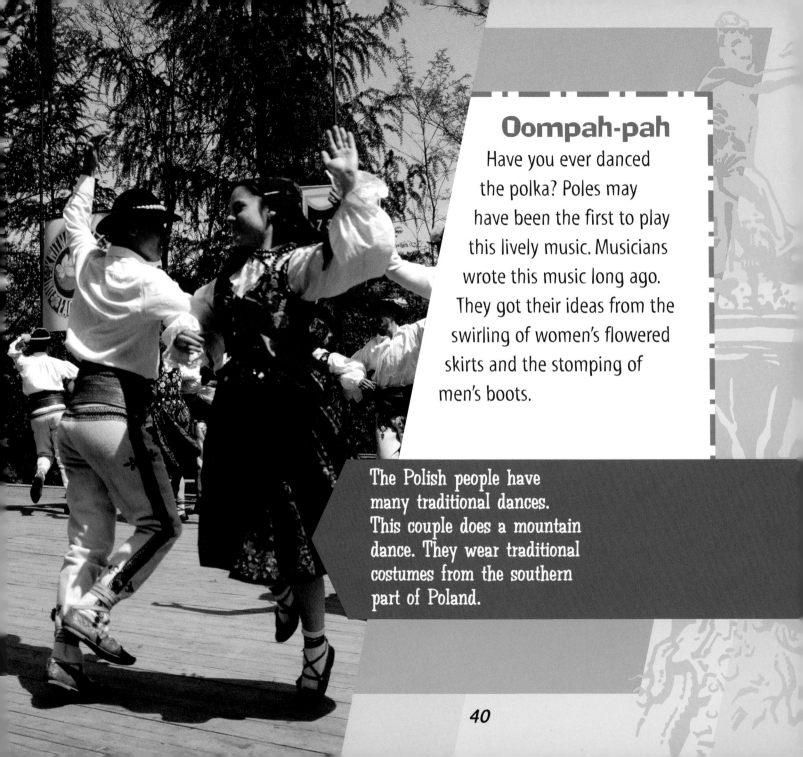

Oompah-pah

Have you ever danced the polka? Poles may have been the first to play this lively music. Musicians wrote this music long ago. They got their ideas from the swirling of women's flowered skirts and the stomping of men's boots.

The Polish people have many traditional dances. This couple does a mountain dance. They wear traditional costumes from the southern part of Poland.

For weddings and festivals, Polish kids practice their polka steps. But most of the time, they dance to pop, rock, and rap music.

These Polish children wear traditional folk costumes.

Polish people enjoy vacationing in the Carpathian Mountains.

Take a Break

Most Polish workers get four weeks of vacation each year. In the wintertime, families might ski in the Carpathian Mountains. Polish kids love sleigh rides in the country.

They have fun in the summertime. Some people take boat rides down the Dunajec River. Fishing and canoeing in the Lake Region are popular too. Some people visit historic places. Others go to folk festivals.

Tourists ride a raft down a tributary of the Vistula River in southern Poland.

THE FLAG OF POLAND

Poland's flag consists of two horizontal stripes of equal length. The upper stripe is white. The lower stripe is red. Red and white were chosen as the national colors in 1831. They were the colors on a Polish kingdom's coat of arms (the symbol standing for a family or kingdom). The flag was adopted by the Polish legislature in 1919. Since 2004, Polish Flag Day is celebrated on May 2.

FAST FACTS

FULL COUNTRY NAME: Republic of Poland

AREA: 120,728 square miles (312,685 square kilometers). That is a little smaller than the state of New Mexico.

MAIN LANDFORMS: the mountain ranges Carpathian and Sudeten; the Polish Uplands; the plains; the forested lake regions; the coastal lowlands.

MAJOR RIVERS: Oder and Vistula

ANIMALS AND THEIR HABITATS: bears, elks, European bison, foxes, and lynx (Bialowieza Forest); mountain deer, wild boars, and wolves (mountain valleys and forests); black storks, cormorants, and wild swans (northern lakes and rivers); and various types of fish (rivers, lakes, and Baltic Sea).

CAPITAL CITY: Warsaw

OFFICIAL LANGUAGE: Polish

POPULATION: about 38,621,000

GLOSSARY

capital: a city where the government of a state or country is located

Communist: a system of government in which the state owns all or most businesses and property

continent: any one of seven large areas of land. The continents are Africa, Antarctica, Asia, Australia, Europe, North America, and South America.

ethnic group: a group of people with many things in common, such as language, religion, and customs

ethnic Poles: people from an early Slavic group called the Polanie. Ethnic Poles are the largest ethnic group in Poland.

invade: to enter by force and attack

map: a drawing or chart of all or part of Earth or the sky

mountains: a part of Earth's surface that rises high into the sky

plains: a large area of flatland

Slav: a member of an ethnic group that came from central Asia and later moved into parts of eastern Europe

tradition: a way of doing things—such as preparing a meal, celebrating a holiday, or making a living—that a group of people have practiced for a long time

TO LEARN MORE

BOOKS

Monte, Richard. *The Dragon of Krakow: And Other Polish Stories.* London: Frances Lincoln Children's Books, 2008.

Polish Children's Picture Dictionary: English-Polish, Polish-English. New York: Hippocrene Books, 2006.

Zamojska-Hutchins, Danuta. *Cooking the Polish Way.* Minneapolis: Lerner Publications Company, 2002.

Zullo, Allan, and Mara Bovsun. *Survivors: True Stories of Children in the Holocaust.* New York: Scholastic, 2005.

WEBSITES

Christmas in Poland
http://www.polishworld.com/christmas
This site introduces Christmas traditions in Poland. You can even send a Polish Christmas postcard over the Internet.

For the Children: Polish-American Heritage Database
http://info-poland.buffalo.edu/classroom/children/intro.html
This site provides a general introduction to Polish history and culture.

Poland in the Classroom
http://wings.buffalo.edu/info-poland
This site provides textual and graphic material on various topics for children.

Polish Culture and History
http://www.polandforvisitors.com/travel_poland/culture_history
Poland has a rich history and culture, dating back more than a thousand years. Meet famous Polish people and learn about Polish culture, lifestyle, and food.

INDEX